-3106

Animal Survivors of the Arctic

Barbara A. Somervill

Franklin Watts
A Division of Scholastic Inc.
New York • Toronto • London • Auckland • Sydney
Mexico City • New Delhi • Hong Kong
Danbury, Connecticut

For Hope and Harold, who taught me that learning is a lifelong opportunity

Note to readers: Definitions for words in **bold** can be found in the Glossary at the back of this book.

Photographs © 2004: AP/Wide World Photos: 44 (Jim Lavrakas), 15, 42; Bruce Coleman Inc.: 25 (Ken Graham); Corbis Images: 32 (Bettmann), 30 (Steve Kaufman), 5 right, 16, 19, 21, 49 (Galen Rowell); Dembinsky Photo Assoc./Dominique Braud: 6; Folio, Inc./David Falconer: 10; ImageState/ Kennan Ward Photography: 2, 22; Peter Arnold Inc.: 13 (Steve Kaufman), 38 (Fritz Polking); Photo Researchers, NY: cover, 12, 27, 40 (B & C Alexander), 29 (Dan Guravich), 35 (Steve Krasemann), 5 left, 9, 34, 46 (Yva Momatiuk & John Eastcott); Visuals Unlimited: 50 (George Herbew), 11 (Maslowski); Woodfin Camp & Associates/Momatiuk/Eastcott: 37.

The photograph on the cover shows a walrus. The photograph opposite the title page shows a couple of polar bears out hunting for food.

Library of Congress Cataloging-in-Publication Data

Somervill, Barbara A.
      Animal Survivors of the Arctic / by Barbara A. Somervill.
         p. cm. — (Watts library)
      Summary: Explores how certain Arctic animals, such as the northern fur seal and the musk ox, have recovered after being threatened with extinction.
      Includes bibliographical references and index.
      ISBN 0-531-12204-2 (lib. bdg.)   0-531-16592-2 (pbk.)
      1. Zoology—Arctic regions—Juvenile literature. 2. Endangered species—Arctic regions—Juvenile literature. [1. Zoology—Arctic regions. 2. Endangered species. 3. Wildlife conservation. 4. Arctic regions.] I. Title. II. Series.
QL105.S66 2004
590'.9113—dc22

                2003012580

Contents

Chapter One
The Frozen North   7

Chapter Two
Arctic Peregrines   17

Chapter Three
Saving the Polar Bears   23

Chapter Four
Northern Fur Seals   31

Chapter Five
Walrus: Arctic Toothwalkers   39

Chapter Six
Tundra Musk Oxen   45

52 **Glossary**

56 **To Find Out More**

60 **A Note on Sources**

61 **Index**

Thick fur, called qiviut, protects musk oxen from winter winds on the Arctic tundra.

Chapter One

The Frozen North

Snow swirls on the **Arctic** wind. It is September, and winter rushes its arrival. Caribou head south along narrow paths through the **tundra**, or land where the ground is permanently frozen. They follow routes used by herds for centuries.

Musk oxen paw the ground as they look for **lichens** and mosses. They will pass the winter on the tundra, despite temperatures that may fall to almost 50 to 60 degrees below 0 degrees Fahrenheit (-46 to -51° Celsius). Bitter winds can reach speeds of up to 100 miles (160 kilometers) per hour.

The changing seasons have sent most birds south to the Gulf Coast or to Mexico. Only a few birds, such as the snowy owl and the ptarmigan, can survive an Arctic winter. Birds are not the only ones heading south, however. Whales, seals, and sea lions also swim south to winter feeding areas.

This is the frozen North—the land of the polar bear and the walrus. Here, the Arctic bustles with animals that brave bitter winters and thrive in all-too-short summers.

Tundra and Permafrost

The Arctic is made up of several different **ecosystems**: tundra, forest, and coastal. Despite the harsh climate, the Arctic feeds and houses millions of animals that could not live anywhere else. Tundra animals range from tiny mosquitoes and flies to massive polar bears. Small mammals, such as snow hares and ground squirrels, spend winter months hidden in deep burrows under the snow, safe from hungry Arctic foxes.

Tundra covers almost 20 percent of Earth's land. Greenland, Canada, the United States, Russia, and Sweden have tundra regions. For many months, tundra soil is frozen solid. Spring thaws only melt the ground from 3 to 20 inches (8 to 50 centimeters) deep. Below this zone lies **permafrost**, or permanently frozen earth. The permafrost layer ranges from 1,300 to 2,000 feet (400 to 600 meters) deep.

Tundra may have very few trees, but it is not barren. About 500 varieties of moss and 450 flowering plants, shrubs, and

Safe on the Tundra

The Arctic National Wildlife Refuge (ANWR), in Alaska's far northeastern corner, is a vast **preserve** on the tundra. The refuge shelters one of the largest caribou herds in the world. Wolf packs, grizzly bears, wolverines, Dall sheep, and musk oxen live on land as clean and undisturbed today as it was ten million years ago. Millions of birds nest in ANWR each summer. Snow geese, tundra swans, golden plovers, and Arctic loons raise their young in the short summers of ANWR.

ferns live there. Low-lying willows and birches line the river-banks. Bearberry and crowberry shrubs provide fruit for Arctic birds. Warm summer sun brings bright buttercups, orange poppies, and blue harebells that dance in the gentle breeze. Plants depend on rivers for most of their water because precipitation on the tundra is low. An average year sees less than 10 inches (25 cm) of rain, snow, or sleet.

The **tree line** is a strip of land that separates the tundra from the forestland. Short trees and shrubs grow in thin clusters along the tree line. Below the tree line lies the **taiga**, an area of dense evergreen woodland. Songbirds and **raptors** find shelter amid stands of aspen, tamarack, and spruce trees. Each summer, wild asters, lupines, and larkspur paint taiga meadows with lively colors. By August, crowberry and soapberry shrubs burst with fruit for brown bears and songbirds to eat.

The tundra holds snowmelt in temporary ponds. The melted water does not sink into the ground because the earth is permanently frozen.

Icebergs and floes break away, or calve, from mainland glaciers.

On the Arctic coastline, whales, walrus, polar bears, and seals breed and raise their young near or on the shore during the summer months. In winter, Arctic seas freeze over. Polar bears depend on solid **pack ice** for hunting. They search for seals' breathing holes, then wait for their prey to come up to the surface of the ice. At the edge of the solid ice, flat icebergs or **floes** drift along with the current. Seals and walrus gather on these floes in the bright Arctic sun.

Keystone Species: Caribou and Ringed Seals

Keystone species describes a plant or animal vital to an ecosystem. Without that **species**, other plants and animals could not survive. Two keystone species live in the Arctic: caribou and ringed seals.

Twice yearly, large caribou herds **migrate** across the open Arctic plains. As they follow one behind the other, the caribou carve deep paths in the land. They not only reshape the land but also fulfill a role in the **food chain**. Reshaping the land can be both good and bad. Well-worn paths can direct or collect rainwater for animals to drink. But heavy traffic over an area can damage or wear away soil. The eroded soil builds up along the sides of the caribou paths. The soil banks provide rich beds for plant growth. Unfortunately, the topsoil is only a few inches deep. Plants that spread along their roots do not cross caribou paths. There is not enough soil to carry the roots, and hard permafrost blocks the way. Root-spreading plants provide valuable food for the caribou, and the erosion of topsoil reduces the caribou food supply.

Polar bears, wolves, and birds of prey feed on weak and newborn caribou. The remaining carcasses also provide food for **rodents** and insects. Antlers that caribou have shed become a mineral source for porcupines.

Caribou herds follow the same paths at the same time each year. Native people of the region could tell the changing seasons and plan their hunts by the caribou migration.

Ringed seals provide food for polar bears, although the bears eat only the seal blubber. Other animals, such as Arctic foxes, wolves, and ravens, eat the remaining meat and bones.

Caribou also expand plant **populations**. Herds feed on willow leaves, lichens, and flowering plants. Their **feces** spread plant seeds and spores as the herd moves from place to place.

Like the caribou, ringed seals are essential to their Arctic ecosystem. The ringed seal is the main food of polar bears. Polar bears eat only the blubber of the seal, however. Muscle, bones, and organs are left behind. Foxes, walrus, dogs, wolves, wolverines, and ravens consume the ringed seals' remains and depend on this species for survival.

A Wilderness in Danger

The Arctic environment seems rugged enough to survive a great deal of damage, but it can't. The soil layer is thin and fragile. Wind, water, and animal travel erode Arctic soil, reducing plant growth.

Erosion is not the only **environmental** problem. Mining natural resources, **pollution**, **global warming**, and even building projects affect delicate Arctic ecosystems. Oil drilling and mining of gold and silver threaten natural **habitats**. Mining requires people and machinery, along with power sources and supplies. Every project needs roads, processing plants, and housing. All of this development means pollution, garbage, and soil damage. Plans for oil drilling in ANWR, for example, could damage caribou and polar bear habitats.

Global warming concerns **environmentalists**. As Earth warms, polar ice melts and ocean levels rise. Winters become shorter and warmer. Hard pack ice covers the sea for less time. For polar bears hunting on the ice, these changes mean shorter hunting time and a greater chance of starving.

Pollution threatens even the most remote Arctic areas. Wind carries acid rain and chemical pollution, which destroy

Mining operations, such as this one on Faith Creek, Alaska, increase topsoil erosion and damage delicate permafrost.

fragile tundra plants and reduce the amount of food available to grazing animals. Oil spills threaten coastal animals and plants and produce damage that lasts for many years.

Finally, overhunting has seriously reduced the **populations** of bears, whales, seals, and walrus. Animals that supported native cultures in the past have been turned into fur, whale oil, and hunting businesses that tip the balance of nature.

Preserving Wilderness

Today, environmental organizations, native people, and government agencies work to preserve the Arctic wilderness. For example, **ecologists** fight against oil companies that want to drill for oil in ANWR. These organizations are also hard at work to help the animals that make the Arctic their home. In Canada, national parks and preserves in the Northern Territory and other Arctic areas provide safe habitats for musk oxen and caribou. Canadian scientists carefully observe these species, as well as polar bear populations around Churchill, Manitoba.

The Arctic Network links environmental efforts by Denmark, Canada, Finland, Sweden, Russia, Iceland, Norway, and the United States. In addition, the International Whaling Commission oversees whaling **quotas** and bans in Arctic waters. Legal bans on killing fur seals, walrus, and sea lions—except for animals that support native people—save these species for future generations.

Efforts to save **endangered** Arctic species have produced

What You Can Do

If you would like to help preserve the Arctic wilderness, write to your U.S. senators and representatives. Urge them to save wilderness areas.

many success stories. Nature preserves, wilderness areas, and controlled hunting have helped to rescue bears and birds from extinction. Today, mother polar bears teach their cubs to hunt ringed seals. Growing herds of musk oxen roam open Arctic plains. Massive male walrus fight for the right to mate with a **harem** of females. Along the shore, once-threatened northern fur seals thrive as hundreds of new pups bleat in the nursery. A solitary Arctic peregrine falcon glides along on warm summer air. He hunts to feed the hungry chicks in his nest. They, too, now have a chance for survival.

A 90-foot (27-m) inflatable whale marks the site where the International Whaling Commission meets. The group is a committee of forty-three nations that controls whaling worldwide.

15

Peregrine falcon parents hunt continuously to feed their growing chicks. The chicks must be large enough and strong enough to migrate before winter settles on the tundra.

Chapter Two

Arctic Peregrines

A female Arctic peregrine falcon meets her mate in midair above Alaska's Colville River. He has caught a sandpiper, or a type of shorebird, to feed their three ever-hungry young. The male passes the food to the female in-flight, and the mother peregrine heads home to the nest. Her return trip will be a short one—falcons can fly at speeds up to 60 miles (95 km) per hour. The well-fed chicks are strong and active, and they could injure their mother in the rush to feed. She plays it safe and drops the food into the nest from a few feet overhead. These parent falcons are one of more than sixty pairs nesting along the Colville. Their successful breeding offers great hope for the future of their species.

Problems for Arctic Peregrine Falcons

In the early 1940s, use of the **pesticide** DDT all but doomed the Arctic peregrine falcon to **extinction**. In the falcons' winter habitats in Mexico and South America, this pesticide was commonly used to kill crop-eating insects. The insects were,

Arctic Peregrine Falcon Fast Facts

Description:	Bluish-gray upper feathers with pale cream or white on the underbody; Pointed wings, rounded tail; Females are 40 percent heavier than males
Male and Female:	No specific name
Offspring:	Chicks or young, in **clutches** of 2 to 5 eggs
Groups:	Nesting pairs
Maximum Life Span:	16 to 20 years
Average Size:	Length, 15 to 21 inches (0.4 to 0.5 m); weight, is 1.3 to 2.3 pounds (0.6 to 1 kg).
Wingspan:	3 to 4 feet (about 1 to 1.2 m)
Food:	Birds, bats, mice, insects, and small rodents
Range/Habitat:	Nest and breed in North American tundra; winter in coastal regions and mountains of Florida, the Gulf Coast, Mexico, southern California, and South America.

in turn, eaten by songbirds and wading birds—the prey of peregrine falcons. Arctic peregrines prey on gulls, terns, swifts, flickers, and jays. With every successful hunt, the falcons consumed more poison.

While the amount of the poison did not directly kill the falcons, it created a different, greater threat. The DDT caused falcons to lay eggs with shells that were too thin to produce healthy chicks. The eggs cracked under the weight of a nesting parent, killing the chick inside. In some cases, the amount of poison was great enough to kill chicks outright. The falcon population could not breed successfully.

The shell on the left is the normal thickness for peregrine falcon eggs. The thinner shell on the right came from a falcon exposed to the pesticide DDT.

In the early 1970s, DDT use was banned. By 1975, only nine nesting pairs of Arctic peregrine falcons lived in the Colville River area. In other Arctic habitats, few, if any, falcons survived. To keep the population at the 1975 level, each nesting pair had to produce two chicks that lived to adulthood.

Conservation Efforts

Arctic peregrines, along with other migrating birds, are protected under the Migratory Bird Treaty Acts. The first act was passed in 1918, and it has been changed several times since then. These laws made it illegal to chase, hunt, kill, trap, possess, buy, sell, or trade any migratory bird. The acts included not only the birds themselves but also feathers or bird parts, nests, and eggs. The treaties provided separate agreements between the United States and Great Britain, Mexico, Japan, and Russia.

The Endangered Species Acts of 1969 and 1973 further protected the Arctic peregrine falcon. Officials closely watched nests to prevent people from harvesting chicks for the sport of **falconry**. Similar efforts in Canada and Greenland protected Arctic peregrines.

The peregrine population slowly grew as more chicks hatched and lived to adulthood. Today, thousands of nesting pairs breed in the North American tundra. By 1994, the population reached a large enough number that the Arctic peregrine falcon was removed from the U.S. Fish and Wildlife

Raptors Can Be Good Guys

For many years, farmers believed that raptors, like the Arctic peregrine falcon, were a danger to young farm animals. This is untrue. Raptors actually help farmers by hunting rodents, insects, and songbirds that destroy grain crops.

Falconers use a falcon puppet to feed a chick. They want the chick to bond with other falcons, not humans.

Service's List of Endangered and Threatened Wildlife Species. The recovery plans had been successful.

Although Arctic peregrine falcons are safe in North America, they still face danger on their migration routes. Some countries in Central and South America continue to use pesticides that are similar to DDT. Falcons that winter in these countries may eat prey that has consumed these poisons. It is hoped that the cycle of damaged eggs and unhatched chicks will not repeat itself, and the Arctic peregrine population will grow.

A mother polar bear and her cubs emerge from their den as early spring awakens the Arctic.

Chapter Three

Saving the Polar Bears

Two polar bear cubs emerge from the den under a bright April sky. At birth, they weighed about 2 pounds (0.9 kg) each. They are about the same size as an adult gray squirrel. Now, after three months of their mother's rich milk, they are a hefty 30 pounds (13.6 kg) each.

The landscape is covered with snow and a brilliant white. The cubs' mother built her den on a hillside, and the twins quickly learn how to slide downhill on their bottoms. For the next two years, they will live with their mother and be well fed. During this time, they must learn to scent seals under the ice and to hunt at a breathing hole. Their lives depend on how well they learn these lessons.

Humans, the Greatest Threat

The massive, solitary adult polar bear has no natural enemies except for humans. The polar bear lives on or near Arctic ice. It travels many miles over the ice to hunt for food. As is true for many endangered animals, polar bears are victims of habitat destruction, pollution, and global warming.

Drilling for oil and natural gas along the Arctic Ocean severely damaged the polar bear's natural habitat. Tankers for transporting oil, pipelines, pollution from processing plants, housing developments, and even garbage damage the Arctic and harm the bears. Pollution from oil spills and toxic chemicals also have harmed Arctic food chains. Many small animals carry toxic levels of chemicals like **PCBs** in their bodies. When a bear eats such an animal, it is also eating the poisons in that animal.

The worst problem for polar bears may be global. Pack ice

lasts about three to four fewer weeks than it did twenty-five years ago. In addition, ice in some areas is not as thick as it used to be. Since the primary hunting time for polar bears is when pack ice remains solid, early thaws reduce the amount of food polar bears can eat.

Drilling rigs in the Arctic Ocean increase pollution. They endanger polar bears because the pollution poisons the bear's food supply.

Population Count

It is difficult to determine the exact number of polar bears. They live remote lives in isolated Arctic regions. The current estimate is that 25,000 to 30,000 polar bears live in the United States, Canada, Greenland, Norway, and Russia.

The bears form ten to fifteen separate population groups in

Polar Bear Fast Facts

Description:	The largest bear, with a coat of clear, hollow hair over a dark gray or black skin; the hair reflects sunlight, making it appear white
Male:	Boar
Female:	Sow
Offspring:	1 to 2 cubs every three years
Groups:	Family groups of a mother and cubs
Maximum Life Span:	25 to 30 years
Average Size:	**Male:** height, 7.9 to 8.5 feet (2.4 to 2.6 m); weight 880 to 1,320 pounds (400 to 600 kg) **Female:** height, 6.5 feet (1.9 m); weight 500 pounds (226 kg)
Food:	Ringed seals, bearded seals, harp seals, walrus, and white whales
Range/Habitat:	Arctic Russia, North America, Greenland, and Norway

five countries. Canada's Northwest Territory, for example, is home to three populations with a total of three thousand bears. Yet, following tagged polar bears shows that the bears do not mix among populations.

Native people hunted polar bears for centuries with little damage to the population. Planes and snowmobiles have made hunting for sport easier and more effective. By the 1970s, there were only about eight thousand polar bears remaining, and the species was listed as endangered. It was time to protect the bears from humans.

An International Effort

In 1973, the countries with polar bear populations signed the International Agreement for the **Conservation** of Polar Bears. Polar bear populations grew, but threats continued.

In Norway, polar bears have been protected for almost thirty years. Although the population doubled from one thousand to two thousand bears, pollution remains a concern. For example, PCB levels are two to seventeen times higher in Norwegian and Russian polar bears than in North American animals.

Russia now allows native peoples to hunt polar bears without limit. This encourages **poaching**, or illegal hunting. This is a serious problem that may have long-term effects on the total polar bear population.

Native hunters use all parts of a polar bear. The thick polar bear fur will make a warm parka, line boots, or be used as a blanket.

Canada, the United States, and Greenland allow limited polar bear hunting by native people. This accounts for about seven hundred bears yearly. In Alaska, native people can kill a bear, but they must use the carcass. They are not allowed to sell the skins, but they can make and sell skin products. Greenland natives kill about one hundred bears per year, but they cannot sell any bear parts. Canadian natives receive a quota on polar bear hunting, and they may sell hunting rights to nonnative people. The right to hunt and kill one polar bear costs an "outsider" about $10,000 to $13,000 in U.S. dollars.

The Churchill Problem

Residents of Churchill in the Canadian province of Manitoba have more contact with polar bears than they might like. This Hudson Bay community is the gathering place for polar bears waiting for pack ice to form. Locals avoid polar bears by keeping their garbage indoors and watching out for wandering he-bears. There are times when a particularly hungry or violent bear becomes dangerous. These bears are usually trapped and released far from Churchill. Other times, they must be killed.

On Alaska's North Slope, towns are taking positive action to limit human contact with bears. Says Scott Schliebe of the Marine Mammals Management Field Office, "The first thing is to detect bears in the area. North Slope towns don't trap and release, they haze the bears and chase them away." Detecting and handling bear situations is an important part of public education that protects both people and bears.

Pesky polar bears that gather around Churchill, Canada, are airlifted to a safer location.

In the past thirty years, the polar bear population has almost tripled. Still, growing pollution, loss of habitat, and shorter feeding seasons may eventually take their toll on the polar bear. Paying attention to polar bear populations and conserving habitats are the only ways to keep this Arctic giant safe.

Infant fur seals drink mother's milk, which is rich in fat. They will more than double their birth weight in just a few days.

Chapter Four

Northern Fur Seals

A northern fur seal pup is born on June 17 on Bogoslof Island near Alaska. After a summer in the **rookery**, it is time for the pup to head south for the winter. At just three months old, the pup swims up to 35 miles (60 km) daily on the 1,500-mile (2,500-km) trip to the California coast.

Along the way, the seal pup might fall prey to killer whales or might be caught in broken fishing nets. It will have to feed itself, since fur seal mothers stop

Seal fur was high fashion in the 1920s. Hunting fur seals for their skins nearly drove the species to extinction.

nursing after three months. For much of its life, this seal will live at sea. Fur seals only come on land to breed and to give birth to their young.

History of the Fur Seal Trade

Georg Steller, traveling with a Russian exploration group, first described northern fur seals in 1742. His report said that adults and pups were covered with thick, lush fur—a feature that almost caused their extinction. Russia immediately began harvesting Alaska's fur seals. The government set up trading posts to buy furs. Between 1786 and 1867, hunters killed about 2.5 million seals for their fur. Russian hunting laws of the period protected females and controlled killing rates.

In 1867, the United States bought Alaska from Russia. The Pribilof Islands Area Habitat Conservation Zone became a fur seal preserve in 1869, and the U.S. Treasury licensed seal hunting in other areas. The safety of the Pribilof refuge lasted one year, until the Alaska Commercial Company received a license to hunt seals there. Then, hunters began taking seals straight from the sea, killing them with harpoons and spears. Many seals that escaped the hunters were wounded and died at sea.

In the early 1900s, fur collars, coats, and dress trims were the height of fashion. Hunters killed millions of fur seals for their pelts. Canada, Japan, Russia, and the United States decided to protect fur seals through the North Pacific Fur Seal

Convention of 1911. The agreement lasted thirty years and the seal population rebounded.

By the 1940s, laws limited seal harvests to adult males taken from **haulouts** during breeding season. The northern fur seal's plight never reached endangered levels because protection laws were passed before the situation reached a critical point. Commercial seal hunting stopped completely in the United States and Canada by the mid-1980s. By then, fashions had changed. Many women no longer wore fur on their clothes. Since then, native people have taken about two thousand seals yearly as a **subsistence** harvest.

Today's Population

Because northern fur seals live mostly in the open sea, their population count is a matter of guesswork. In June, adult males arrive at the haulout area. Within a week, females arrive, and new pups are born within days of their mothers hauling out. This is the best time to take a census.

Since the 1960s, new breeding groups of northern fur seals have formed on San Miguel Island and Castle Rock, California, and on Bogoslof Island in the Bering Sea. By 1992, the Bogoslof Island rookery had about 500 pups and a total population of 2,235 seals. In recent years, more than 11,000 northern fur seals lived on San Miguel.

Three-fourths of all northern fur seals live on the Pribilof Islands off the coast of Alaska. The population, once in the millions, has slowly dwindled over the past forty years.

Fur Seal Fast Facts

Description:	Pointed nose; reddish brown to brown-black fur; whiskered snout; side and rear flippers
Male:	Bull
Female:	Cow
Offspring:	1 pup born each year
Groups:	Herd
Maximum Life Span:	About 40 years
Size:	**Male:** length, 80 to 82 inches (2.0 to 2.1 m); weight, 400 to 600 pounds (182 to 272 kg) **Female:** length, 53 to 60 inches (1.4 to 1.5 m); weight, 95 to 110 pounds (43 to 50 kg)
Food:	Herring, pollock, whiting, salmon, and squid
Range/Habitat:	Northern Pacific, Bering Sea, Chukchi Sea

Seals haulout on a beach in the Pribilof Islands off Alaska.

This decline is caused by seals being caught or trapped in fishing nets; commercial fishing, which reduces food supplies; and changing weather patterns. Today, about 982,000 northern fur seals swim in U.S. waters.

Recovery Plans

Northern fur seals are covered under the Marine Mammal Protection Acts of 1972 and 1988. While the acts protect seals and their habitats from people, the laws sometimes prevent efforts to help seals during difficult times. Such was the case when El Niño, an unusual weather pattern, wiped out normal food supplies for seals wintering along the California coast. The seals were starving, but the law stopped groups from feeding and saving them.

This seal is lucky to be alive. When seals get caught in fishing nets, they can not free themselves and often drown.

U.S. and Japanese scientists are studying seal entanglements, which happen when seals are caught in fishing nets and trash. Seals get trapped in trawling nets, plastic packing

It takes a brave hunter to tangle with these huge marine mammals. An adult walrus could easily sink a one-person kayak.

Chapter Five

Walrus: Arctic Toothwalkers

An Inuit hunter leaves for a hunt in a one-person kayak. Alone, he heads into the Bering Sea and searches for ice floes. He spots a large iceberg with more than two dozen walrus on it. He paddles quietly toward them. If he disturbs them, the animals might slip into the water and dive down out of reach.

The hunter sneaks closer and harpoons a calf. This year, the hunter has harvested a female and two calves. The harvest will keep his family alive through

Once a walrus has been slain, the community works together to prepare the blubber and meat.

the winter. The meat feeds his family and the dogs that pull his dogsled. Inuit use bone for making tools; skins for waterproof boats, sleds, and clothing; and blubber for fuel oil.

Native people have hunted walrus for centuries without damaging the walrus population. However, walrus cannot survive mass hunting, commercial fishing, and loss of habitat.

Conservation Issues

Issues that plague other sea mammals also harm the walrus. For example, walrus eat marine animals that may be affected by pollution. They also suffer from loss of habitat, global warming, and overhunting.

Walrus eat clams, snails, worms, and shrimp, all of which live along the sea floor. These animals are often found in coastal waters—areas that are more likely than deep seas to be affected by pollution. Oil spills, chemical spills, and garbage increase pollution levels near the shore. If pollution does not kill marine animals outright, toxins remain in the animals and walrus eat those toxins.

How Old Is This Walrus?

As with a tree, the number of rings in a cross-section of a walrus tusk tells the animal's age. New tooth growth happens yearly for walrus.

Oil drilling, building projects, and noise near haulout areas hinder breeding. If human activity is too lively, a **beachmaster**—the dominant male walrus—will keep his harem at sea instead of landing for breeding.

Walrus spend their time on free-floating ice. They haul themselves up onto ice floes with their long tusks. From this, they get the name "toothwalker." As summer comes and large floes melt, walrus herds move northward. Global warming reduces the amount of loose pack ice, thus decreasing the walrus' habitat.

The greatest threat to the walrus, however, was commercial hunting. Since the mid-1800s, the Pacific walrus population has rebounded from overhunting three times. Like the

Walrus Fast Facts

Description:	Long tusks on males and females; thick, bumpy skin; small head, eyes, and nose; sensitive whiskers; side and rear flippers
Male:	Bull
Female:	Cow
Offspring:	1 calf born every 2 to 3 years
Groups:	Herd
Maximum Life Span:	16 to 30 years
Average size:	**Male:** length, 9 to 12 feet (2.7 to 3.6 m); weight, 1,764 to 3,748 pounds (800 to 1,700 kg) **Female:** length, 7.5 to 10 feet (2.3 to 3.1 m); weight, 882 to 2,756 pounds (400 to 1,250 kg)
Food:	Clams, snails, crabs, shrimp, and worms
Range/Habitat:	Polar seas around Alaska, Canada, Greenland, and Russia

fur seal, the walrus never reached endangered or threatened status because controls prevented further population decline. Today, only native hunters may harvest walrus. According to Carl Kava, of the Eskimo Walrus Commission, "Native hunting has a limited impact on walrus populations because basic hunting techniques have changed very little since the 1800s."

Managing the Walrus Population

Of the approximately 250,000 walrus in the world, about 200,000 live in the northern Pacific Ocean, Bering Sea, and Chukchi Sea. The remaining 50,000 live in the North Atlantic Ocean, around Canada and Greenland.

Today, the U.S. Fish and Wildlife Service manages walrus living in U.S. waters. This agency runs population counts, oversees harvests, and protects the walrus population. One of the agency's current projects is to plan a new walrus census. This is a difficult task. Walrus often lie on top of each other. They also spend plenty of time in water and moving around, which causes scientists to count too many or too few. A walrus census is, at best, a good guess. Scientists hope that using body-heat scans will produce a more accurate count.

In the 1970s, Alaskan natives started the Eskimo Walrus Commission (EWC). The EWC

A scientist tracks the movements of walrus in Alaskan waters. Each year, he spends two weeks attaching new transmitters to walruses for this purpose.

strives to limit walrus hunting to native cultures and to ensure that walrus do not become **extinct**.

Among the tasks of the EWC is overseeing subsistence hunts. The group encourages native hunters to follow rules for walrus hunting, including using safe hunting methods. In many villages, many native families could not survive without harvesting walrus.

Ongoing Efforts

During periods when commercial hunting stops, the walrus population usually thrives. Recently, however, native hunters have reported changes in the walrus population. It appears that fewer calves are being born.

Scientists who study walrus population trends have noted this lower birth rate. A survey of the Chukchi Sea walrus population shows that the ratio of young calves to adults is lower than it should be. Russian and U.S. scientists hope to discover reasons and solutions for lower calving rates.

In Canada, walrus management falls under the Department of Fisheries and Oceans. This group focuses on reducing waste from killed walrus and controlling the number of animals harvested each year. Waste can happen when an animal is killed only for its ivory or when a walrus dies and sinks before the carcass is collected. Efforts by the Canadian government are underway to reduce both situations. Only careful management can help guarantee that the walrus will thrive in their Arctic habitat.

Marine Mammal Protection Acts

The Marine Mammal Protection Acts of 1972 and 1988 make it illegal to bother, hunt, or harm marine mammals in any way. The laws prohibit the buying and selling of parts of these animals, including meat, blubber, or ivory, except by native people.

This newborn musk ox will be on its feet within minutes after birth. He is born with a thick fur coat that can withstand an Arctic blizzard.

Chapter Six

Tundra Musk Oxen

The temperature falls to –20° F (–29° C) on Russia's Siberian tundra. A musk ox cow delivers her calf, and, despite the cold, it survives. Within minutes, the calf gets to its feet and begins nursing from its mother. The calf is born with thick fur, which guards it from the bitter cold.

In the distance, a wolf howls. The musk oxen herd quickly circles around to protect its young. The bulls face forward with their horns pointing toward the enemy. Musk oxen will fight—and defeat—a grizzly bear twice their size to keep newborn calves safe.

Fur on the Hoof

Musk oxen are grazers, like cows and buffaloes. They thrive on grasses that they find beneath deep winter snows.

Ninety thousand years ago, herds of musk oxen crossed the land bridge between Asia and North America. They spread across North America, reaching as far south as Kansas and eastward to Greenland. The musk ox and the caribou are the only hoofed mammals that survived the last great Ice Age.

The musk ox—called *oomingmak*, or bearded one by the Inuit—is an odd-looking animal. It looks like a cross between a water buffalo and a woolly mammoth. Its double fur layer keeps the animal warm, even at temperatures as low as –70° F (–57° C). The inner layer has 4 inches (10 cm) of soft, dense fur, called qiviut, which is eight times warmer than wool. The shaggy outer layer hangs almost to the ground.

The musk ox has few natural enemies. Although preyed upon by wolves and bears, herds thrive on the remote tundra. Extremely bad weather can threaten a herd's survival, however. Musk oxen are **herbivores**, or plant eaters. They eat willow leaves, flowers, and grasses in spring and summer, and they live on mosses and lichens during snow season. When snow becomes too deep, musk oxen have difficulty clearing it away to find food and can starve.

Hunting the Musk Ox

Native people ignored the musk ox, only hunting the animals when caribou or salmon were unavailable. That changed in the mid-1700s, when Europeans arrived in Arctic North America. Herds of musk oxen were sitting ducks for hunters. When threatened, they huddled in a circle, which made hunting easy.

As with buffalo on the Great Plains, hunters killed musk oxen for sport. The meat became standard dinner fare for hunters, explorers, and whalers. In *Wildlife in America*, author Peter Matthiessen says, "An estimated six hundred musk

An Odd Enemy

One Arctic animal poses a serious danger to the musk ox. It's not a bear or a wolf—it's a mosquito. These insects attack the musk ox on its only unprotected spot: the nose. Mosquitoes bite animals or humans and can pick up diseases, which they transfer to their next victims. Musk oxen do not have natural defenses against some of these diseases. Most musk oxen are more likely to die from a disease-infected mosquito bite than from a bear or wolf attack.

Musk Ox Fast Facts

Description:	A short, hoofed mammal with a thick, shaggy brown coat; heavy, curved horns spread across the forehead
Male:	Bull
Female:	Cow
Offspring:	1 to 2 calves, usually every other year
Groups:	Herd
Maximum Life Span:	Up to about 20 years
Average size:	**Male:** height at shoulder, 4 to 5 feet (1.2 to 1.5 m); weight, 600 to 800 pounds (273 to 364 kg) **Female:** height at shoulder, 3.5 to 4 feet (1.1 to 1.2 m); weight, 400 to 500 pounds (182 to 227 kg)
Food:	Grasses, willow leaves, Arctic flowers, mosses, and lichens
Range/Habitat:	Greenland, North American tundra, and Russia

ox[en] were killed for food by Admiral Peary's expeditions to the Arctic alone." In 1865, the last Alaskan musk ox in Alaska was killed near Wainwright. Musk oxen also became extinct in Russia due to overhunting.

By 1900, the musk ox teetered on the brink of extinction. At this point, only a few musk oxen remained in Canada and Greenland. In 1917, the Canadian government passed a law to protect the musk ox. Ten years later, Canada's Thelon Game Sanctuary became the first preserve specifically for musk oxen. Hunting musk oxen and selling hides were strictly forbidden.

Building New Herds

Efforts to establish new herds in Alaska and Russia have succeeded. In 1930, the U.S. Department of the Interior decided to reintroduce musk oxen to Alaska. Greenland sold the United States thirty-four young, healthy musk oxen. These animals formed a central herd that eventually was established on Nunivak Island, Alaska. The herd thrived on the island,

Musk oxen on Canada's Thelon Game Sanctuary enjoy protection from human hunters—but not from tundra wolf packs.

Adopt a Musk Ox

The Musk Ox Farm in Palmer, Alaska, supports the only tame musk ox herd in the world. Through this nonprofit group, private citizens can "adopt" or support a shaggy calf. The calf stays on the farm, and the adoption fee pays for food and care for the calf. Contact the Musk Ox Farm at http://www.muskoxfarm.org.

where food was plentiful, and there were no wolves or bears to prey on the animals.

By 1968, the island population numbered more than seven hundred animals, more than the habitat could support. A plan was formed to start new herds on nearby Nelson Island, Barter Island, in areas near Nome and Cape Thompson, and in the Arctic National Wildlife Reserve. Over the next several years, small groups of one-year-old and young adult musk oxen traveled to their new homes. Under government protection, these herds blossomed.

The musk ox, once lost to the Alaskan Arctic, had been successfully reintroduced. Russian and U.S. scientists hoped that the experiment at Nunivak could be repeated in Russia. In 1975, forty animals were airlifted from the Nunivak herd to Russia. Musk oxen, which had roamed the Russian tundra for nearly one million years, had returned home.

Once the species was protected from hunters, the population increased dramatically. Alaska now has a musk ox population of more than 2,500 animals. Worldwide population estimates range from 65,000 to 85,000 animals. The musk oxen success story shows that reintroducing a species into its former ecosystem can work if that species is protected.

Glossary

Arctic—the region between the North Pole and the Arctic Circle, an imaginary line at 66° 30' north

beachmaster—a male seal or walrus that has control over a herd of females

clutch—a set of eggs laid by one female bird

conservation—protecting animals, plants, and natural resources from harm

ecologist—a person who studies how living things interact with their surroundings and with each other

ecosystem—a group of plants and animals that form a distinct community

endangered—at risk of disappearing from the earth

environmental—having to do with outside factors that affect living things

environmentalist—a person who studies how outside factors affect living things

extinct—describing an organism that no longer exists

extinction—the state of no longer existing

falconry—the sport of training falcons to hunt

feces—solid bodily waste

floe—a block of floating ice

food chain—a series of living things that are connected because each item is food for the being that follows it

global warming—a trend of higher air temperatures that affects climate

habitat—the place where a plant or animal is naturally found

harem—a group of female animals kept together for breeding purposes

haulout—a beach area where seals and walrus come on land

herbivore—a plant-eating animal

keystone species—a plant or animal species vital to an ecosystem

lichen—a type of fungus

migrate—to travel long distances between a winter and summer home

pack ice—sea ice that has been pushed together to form a mass

PCBs—toxic chemicals used in electrical parts

permafrost—a permanently frozen layer of soil in the tundra

pesticide—a chemical used to kill insects and rodents

poaching—illegal hunting of animals

pollution—a substance responsible for making something dirty or impure

population—the number of beings in a group

pregnant—having unborn young growing in the body

preserve—land protected by the government

quota—a fixed amount

raptor—a bird of prey

rodent—a member of the rat family

rookery—a nursery for seals, sea lions, and walrus

species—a group of like plants or animals that can breed and produce young

subsistence—having just enough to live, as in hunting seals or walrus to provide food, hides, and oil

taiga—an area of thick evergreen forestland

tree line—a ribbon of land separating tundra from forestland

tundra—a vast, treeless plain in the Arctic

To Find Out More

Books

Curlee, Lynn. *Into the Ice: The Story of Arctic Exploration*. Boston: Houghton, 1998.

Dutemple, Lesley A. *Seals and Sea Lions*. San Diego: Lucent Books, 1999.

Patent, Dorothy Hinshaw. *Great Ice Bear: The Polar Bear and the Eskimo*. New York: William Morrow & Company, 1999.

Pipes, Rose. *Tundra and Cold Deserts*. Austin, TX: Raintree/Steck Vaughn, 1999.

Rau, Dana Meachen, and Peg Magovern. *Arctic Adventure: Inuit Life in the 1800s*. Washington, D.C.: Smithsonian, 1997.

Shepard, Donna Walsh. *Alaska*. Danbury, CT: Children's Press, 1999.

Stewart, Melissa. *Seals, Sea Lions, and Walruses*. Danbury, CT: Franklin Watts, 2001.

Videos

Alaska's Arctic Wildlife. Bo and Elizabeth Boudart. ASIN: 0967712637. 1997.

Arctic Kingdom: Life at the Edge. ASIN: 079229808X. 1996.

Toothwalkers: Giants of the Arctic Ice. ASIN: 6305072493. 1998.

Organizations and Online Sites

Alaska Department of Natural Resources
400 Willoughby, 5th floor
Juneau, AK 99801
This state source oversees rivers, land, and Alaskan coastal regions.

Alaska Natural Heritage Program
University of Alaska
Anchorage, AK 99501
This university program works to preserve Alaska's plant and animal life.

Animal Bytes: Walrus

http://www.seaworld.org.AnimalBytes/walrusab.html

Learn everything you ever needed to know about walruses.

Arctic Peregrines

http://refuges.fws.gov/birds/arcticperegrinefalcon.html

Use this resource to find out about the recovery program for Arctic peregrine falcons.

Marine Mammal Research Group
Box 6244
Victoria, British Columbia,
Canada V8P 5L5

This group of scientists studies whales, dolphins, seals, sea lions, and walrus.

The Musk Ox Farm

http://www.muskoxfarm.org

Learn about a program to raise musk oxen like cattle.

NOAA Fisheries
Alaska Regional Office
P. O. Box 21668
Juneau, AK 99802-1668

This group of fisheries works together to preserve marine life in Alaskan waters.

Peregrine Fund
World Center for Birds of Prey
5666 West Flying Hawk Lane
Boise, ID 83709
The Peregrine Fund is the best source for information about birds of prey.

Polar Bears
http://www.polarbearsalive.org/
This site provides in-depth coverage of polar bears across the Arctic.

A Note on Sources

This book is written to congratulate conservation successes. Research about the Arctic began on the Internet at web sites hosted by U.S. Fish and Wildlife Service, The Nature Conservancy, and the American Zoo Association. *National Geographic* and *Smithsonian* magazines featured excellent articles on Arctic animals.

Also, recognized experts offered current, accurate information on walrus, northern fur seals, and Arctic peregrine falcons. A sincere thanks to the U.S. Fish and Wildlife Service, Mark Webber and Scott Schliebe of the Marine Mammals Management Field Office (Anchorage), and Carl Kava of the Eskimo Walrus Commission for providing up-to-date information for this book.

The organizations in the To Find Out More section can help you with added material about Arctic animals. The material they provide is thorough, informative, and easy-to-read.

—Barbara Somervill

Index

Numbers in *italics* indicate illustrations.

Arctic National Wildlife
    Refuge (ANWR), 8, 13,
    14, 50
Arctic Network, 14

Bogoslof Island, 31, 33

Caribou, 10–12, *11*, 13
Churchill, Manitoba, 14, 28,
    29
Colville River, 17, 18, 20
Commercial fishing, 37, 40

DDT, 18–20, *19*
Department of Fisheries and
    Oceans, 43

Endangered Species Acts, 20
Eskimo Walrus Commission
    (EWC), 42–43

Faith Creek, Alaska, *13*
Falconry, 20, *21*
Floes, 10, *10*
Food chain, 11, 24
Fur seals, *30*, *34*, *35*, *37*
    entanglements, 35–36, *35*
    food, 34, 37
    fur, *32*, *32*
    habitat, 34
    haulouts, 33, 34, 36
    hunting, 32, 33, 36
    life span, 34
    population, 33, 35, 36, 37
    pups, *30*, 31–32, 33, 34,
        37
    rookeries, 31, 33, 36
    size, 34

Global warming, 13, 24, 40,
    41

Icebergs, 10, *10*
International Agreement for the Conservation of Polar Bears, 27
International Whaling Commission, 14, *15*
Inuit people, 24, 39–40, *40*, 43, 47

Keystone species, 10–12

Lichens, 7, 12, 47

Marine Mammal Protection Acts, 35, 36, 43
Matthiessen, Peter, 47–48
Migratory Bird Treaty Acts, 20
Mining, 13, *13*
Mosquitoes, 47
Mosses, 7, 47
Musk Ox Farm, 50, *50*
Musk oxen, *6*, *44*, *46*, *49*, *50*
   calves, *44*, 45, 48
   food, *46*, 47, 48
   fur, *6*, *44*, 45, 47
   habitat, 48
   herds, 15, 49–50, 51
   horns, 45–46
   hunting, 47, 48

life span, 48
mosquito bites, 47
population, 50, 51
size, 48

North Pacific Fur Seal Convention (1911), 32–33, 36
Nunivak Island, 49–50

Oil drilling, 13, 14, 24, *25*, 41
Optimum Sustainable Population (OSP), 36

Pack ice, 10, 24–25
Palmer, Alaska, 50
PCBs, 24
Peregrine falcons, *16*, *21*
   chicks, *16*, 18, 19–20, 21, *21*
   eggs, 19, 21
   flight speed, 17
   food, 17–18
   habitat, 18–19
   life span, 18
   migration, 21
   population, 20
   prey, 17
   size, 18

wingspan, 18
Permafrost, 8, 11
Pesticides, 18–20, *19*, 21
Polar bears, *22*, 27, *29*
 cubs, 15, *22*, 23–24, 26
 dens, *22*, 23
 food, 12, 24, 26
 habitat, 13, 24, 26, 29
 hunting, 26, 27–28, *27*
 legends, 24
 life span, 26
 population, 25–26, 27, 29
 pregnancy, 24
 size, 26
Pollution, 13–14, 24, *25*, 29, 40
Preserves, 8, 14, 15, 32, 48, *49*
Pribilof Islands, 32, 33, *34*, 35, 36

Qivuit, *6*, 47

Ringed seals, 10, 12, *12*, 15
Rookeries, 31, 33, 36

Schliebe, Scott, 28
Steller, Georg, 32

Taiga, 9
Thelon Game Sanctuary, 48, *49*
Tree line, 9
Tundra, 7, 8, 9, *9*, 45, 51

U.S. Department of the Interior, 49
U.S. Fish and Wildlife Service, 21, 42
U.S. Treasury, 32

Walrus, *38*, *40*
 beachmasters, 41
 breeding, 41
 calves, 39–40, 41, 43
 food, 41
 habitat, 40, 41
 hunting, 39–40, *40*, 41, 42, 43
 life span, 41
 population, 40, 41, 42–43
 size, 41
 tusks, 40, 41
Wildlife in America (Peter Matthiessen), 47–48

About the Author

Barbara Somervill is a true fan of *National Geographic*. She watches their television programs, reads its books, and has *National Geographic*–produced maps all over the house. A special on Arctic wildlife drew her attention to the plight of polar bears, the mass of migrating herds of caribou, and the woes of being a walrus.

Freelance writing keeps Barbara busy. She writes books for children, video scripts, magazine articles, and textbooks. Her strangest project ever was a video script about coffins!

Barbara was raised and educated in New York. She has also lived in Toronto, Canada; Canberra, Australia; California; and South Carolina. She is an avid reader and traveler and enjoys learning new things every day. Her next trip, she hopes, will be a summertime cruise to Alaska.